THE
FRIENDS
of the
Beverly Hills
Public Library

The
FRESHWATER
Alphabet Book

by Jerry Pallotta

**illustrated by
David Biedrzycki**

Charlesbridge

This book is dedicated to my children, Justin, Alec, and Julia, and their awesome mom, Kathleen.
– David Biedrzycki

The elusive Q fish was discovered through research by Eric Falconer and Gail Huber's students at Central Elementary School in Allison Park, Pennsylvania, and Travis Chambers and Mrs. Newcomer's third graders at Richland Elementary School in Gibsonia, Pennsylvania.
– Jerry Pallotta
Peggotty Beach, 1996

In case you kids are wondering, Biedrzycki rhymes with Icky!
(The e *and the* z *are silent.)*

Published by
Charlesbridge Publishing
85 Main Street, Watertown, MA 02172-4411
(617) 926-0329

Printed in the United States of America
(sc) 10 9 8 7 6 5 4 3 2 1
(hc) 10 9 8 7 6 5 4 3 2 1

Printed on Recycled Paper.

Library of Congress Cataloging-in-Publication Data
Pallotta, Jerry.
    The freshwater alphabet book / by Jerry Pallotta;
illustrated by David Biedrzycki.
        p.   cm.
    ISBN 0-88106-902-7 (library reinforced)
    ISBN 0-88106-901-9 (trade hardcover)
    ISBN 0-88106-900-0 (softcover)
    1. Freshwater biology–Juvenile literature.
2. English language–Alphabet–Juvenile literature. [1.
Freshwater biology. 2. Alphabet.] I. Biedrzycki, David,
ill. II. Title.
QH96.16.P34   1996
574.92'9 – dc20
[E]   95-20138
                                        CIP
                                        AC

Books by Jerry Pallotta:
The Icky Bug Alphabet Book
The Icky Bug Counting Book
The Bird Alphabet Book
The Ocean Alphabet Book
The Flower Alphabet Book
The Yucky Reptile Alphabet Book
The Frog Alphabet Book
The Furry Alphabet Book
The Dinosaur Alphabet Book
The Underwater Alphabet Book
The Victory Garden Vegetable Alphabet Book
The Extinct Alphabet Book
The Desert Alphabet Book
The Spice Alphabet Book
The Butterfly Alphabet Book
Going Lobstering
Cuenta los insectos (The Icky Bug Counting Book)

Oops, we forgot to thank Ichthyologist H.J. Walker!

A a

A is for Amazon River Dolphin. Whales do not live in fresh water, but there are freshwater dolphins. Amazon River Dolphins are only about half as long as their ocean-swimming cousins.

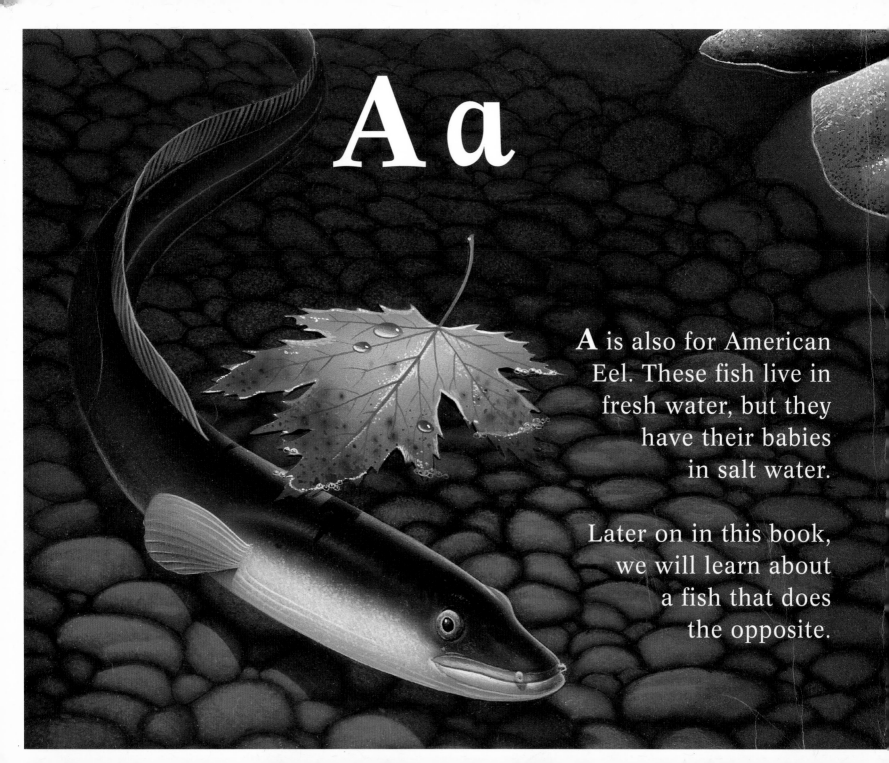

A a

A is also for American Eel. These fish live in fresh water, but they have their babies in salt water.

Later on in this book, we will learn about a fish that does the opposite.

Oh, no! We were trying to get to the **B** page and now this school of fish is in the way.

Bb

B is for Black Molly. Instead of describing the Black Molly, did you know that of all the water on earth, only three percent is fresh water? Humans and Black Mollies cannot live without fresh water. Clean, unpolluted fresh water is precious.

C is for Cavefish. Some cavefish have no eyes, but that's okay. These fish do not need any. They live in caves where there is no sunlight.

Cc

Dd

D is for Dirteater. This fish does not actually eat dirt. It takes pebbles into its mouth, eats the food hidden in the cracks and crevices, and then spits the pebbles back out.

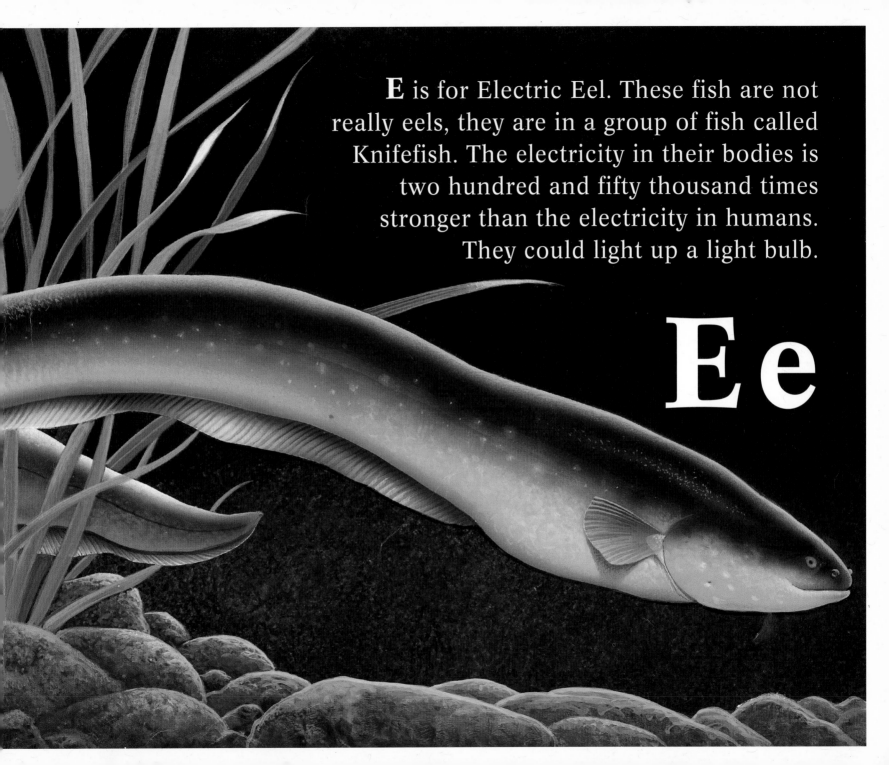

E is for Electric Eel. These fish are not really eels, they are in a group of fish called Knifefish. The electricity in their bodies is two hundred and fifty thousand times stronger than the electricity in humans. They could light up a light bulb.

E e

Ff

F is for Four-eyed Fish. In Spanish it's a Cuatro Ojos. These fish have four retinas which allow them to see above the water and below the water at the same time. Sometimes they swim in brackish water.

G g

G is for Gar. The one on this page is a Longnosed Gar. Fossils have been found which prove that Gars have lived on earth for millions of years. Its scissorlike mouth is excellent for catching other fish.

H h

H is for Halfbeak. It looks like these fish
are upside-down, but they are not.
Halfbeaks are top feeders. It is better
to have a longer lower jaw if your
dinner is near the surface.

I i

I is for Iceworm. Here is a creature that lives in frozen water. ICE! These worms have blood that is like antifreeze. Iceworms live in glaciers, and they eat algae and pollen.

Jj

J is for Jesus Christ Lizard. In South America this amazing reptile is called the Jesus Christ Lizard. It is so fast, and so light, it can run on top of the water. It is also called a Basilisk Lizard.

There it goes! That's one way to clean your feet.

Kk

K is for Koi. You will not find these colorful carp in the wild. People have been fish-farming and cultivating them in Asia for thousands of years. In garden ponds, the exotic Koi are beautiful to watch.

L is for Lamprey. This fish is a parasite. Parasites live off of other plants and animals. The Lamprey attaches its circular mouth to other fish and sucks their blood. Lampreys often leave nasty scars. Yuck! Disgusting!

M m

M is for Mosquitofish. These tiny fish eat the larvae of mosquitoes. We should be thankful, because now there will be less adult mosquitoes buzzing around biting us.

N is for Nessie. Nessie is the nickname of the Loch Ness Monster. Is it real? Many people are convinced it is an ancient plesiosaur trapped in the deep freshwater Scottish lake, Loch Ness. Others think it is a big joke. Some people might even be surprised that this legend is mentioned in a nonfiction book.

O o

O is for Oscar.
Oscars are very popular
with people who have
freshwater aquariums. Oscars
have been known to follow a
person as they walk around the tank.

P is for Paddlefish. An Ichthyologist is a man or woman who studies fish. A Paddlefish is a great fish to study. It has small eyes, smooth skin, sharklike fins, and an unusual nose. This toothless fish eats by straining water through its gill rakers.

Q q

Q is for Quillback. Quillbacks have sharp spines. You can run your finger along its back from the nose to the tail and it will feel smooth. If you run your finger from the tail to the nose— Ouch!

R is for Ricefish. Ricefish are small, but not as small as a grain of rice. They got their name because they can be found swimming in rice paddies.

Rr

S s

S is for Snow Monkey. Snow Monkeys are the only primates besides human beings that have found a way to adapt to cold climates. They survive by living around hot springs.

T is for Trout. On the cover of
this book is a Rainbow Trout. Most
Trout have great names like Lake
Trout, Steelhead, Dolly Varden,
Golden Trout, and Brook Trout.
Some people fly-fish for
Trout, and when they
catch one they kiss it
and then let it go.

T t

U u

It is time to write a letter.
Writing letters is fun.

Dear Fish,
    You are a Uara!

                Sincerely,

                Jerry Pallotta

P.S. I know you are a Uara,
    but what am I?

V v

V is for Veiltail. Veiltails are goldfish with long flowing tails. When they swim, their tails look like flags flapping in the breeze.

W is for Walleye. Walleyes are the biggest fish in their family. Do you know anyone who is the biggest in their family? Other fish in the Walleye family are Logperches and Darters.

W w

X x

Swordtails are on the X page because their scientific name is *Xiphophorus helleri*. **X** is for *Xiphophorus helleri*.

An X-ray Fish, which is not in this book, is a *Pristella maxillaris*.

Y y

Y is for Yabby. Freshwater crustaceans that look like lobsters are called crayfish, crawfish, or crawdads. In Australia, they are called Yabbies. That's right, mate!

Z z

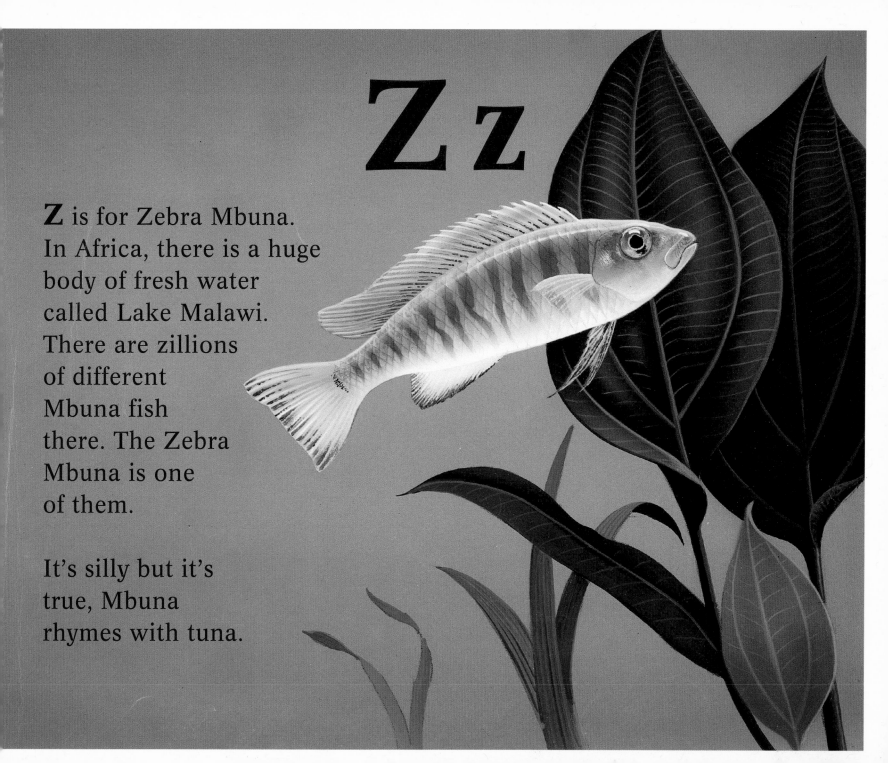

Z is for Zebra Mbuna.
In Africa, there is a huge
body of fresh water
called Lake Malawi.
There are zillions
of different
Mbuna fish
there. The Zebra
Mbuna is one
of them.

It's silly but it's
true, Mbuna
rhymes with tuna.

We are done with the alphabet,
and now, this Salmon is coming home
to the same freshwater stream where it
was born. Most species of Salmon live in
salt water, but they lay their eggs in fresh water.